CRAFTS
Around the House

Janet Skiles

DOVER PUBLICATIONS, INC.
Mineola, New York

Some of my favorite things to do as a child involved creating arts and crafts. Drawing, painting, sorting, cutting, gluing and embellishing kept me entertained for hours. I was also lucky to have a grandmother who was creative and crafty and encouraged me to be the same. Without that early introduction to arts and crafts, I might not have become the professional artist I am today.

The projects in this book have been made using recyclable items from around the house.

Save time by preparing beforehand. Wash bottles, jars, cans, milk cartons, etc., and let them dry before starting your project. Adults may decide to pre-cut, or punch or poke holes with sharp objects, depending upon the skill level of their child. Patterns can be reused if reproduced. Cut them out and have them ready, or help the child cut his or her own patterns. Prepare your workspace with newspaper or a vinyl or plastic tablecloth to make cleanup easier. Place paint in small paper cups, plates, or lids after the child has chosen a few favorite colors. The more time spent on preparation, the more time you can spend having fun with the kids.

Encourage children to let their imaginations flow. Each child is unique and so will be his or her creations. There is no right or wrong in creating, so relax, have fun, make a mess, and make wonderful memories!

—Janet Skiles

Contents

Bibliographical Statement

Crafts Around the House is a new work, first published by Dover Publications, Inc., in 2013.

Manufactured in the United States by Courier Corporation
49759301   2013
www.doverpublications.com

BIRD'S NEST

What you need:

9-inch paper plate
construction paper or foam, variety
    of colors
buttons or wiggle eyes
glue
scissors
brown acrylic paint or crayons
brown paper
popsicle stick for each bird

What to do:

1. Cut a paper plate in half and paint or color each side.
2. Glue the rounded sides or rims together and allow to
   dry, leaving the top open as shown in figure 1 to add the birds.
3. Shred or tear the brown paper and glue pieces to the
   nest as shown in figure 2.
4. Cut out three bird, beak and chest pieces from construction paper
   or foam using the patterns provided on page 3.
5. Glue the eyes, beak, and chest piece to each bird.
6. Glue each bird to a popsicle stick and add to the nest as shown in figure 3.

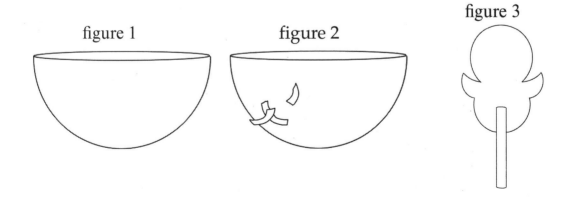

figure 1

figure 2

figure 3

PLASTIC BOTTLE PUPPY

What you need:

plastic soda or water bottle
construction paper or foam
cardboard
acrylic paint and brush
buttons or wiggle eyes
scissors
glue

What to do:

1. Paint the bottle with chosen color and allow to dry thoroughly.
2. Cut out two ears and tail pieces from construction paper or foam using the patterns on page 3.
3. Cut four legs using cardboard for added stability.
4. Glue the legs, ears, and tail to the bottle as shown.
5. Decorate the puppy with painted spots and paint the end of the bottle cap for the nose. Don't forget to add a smile!
6. Glue on the eyes.

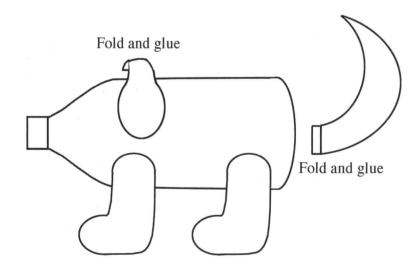

Fold and glue

Fold and glue

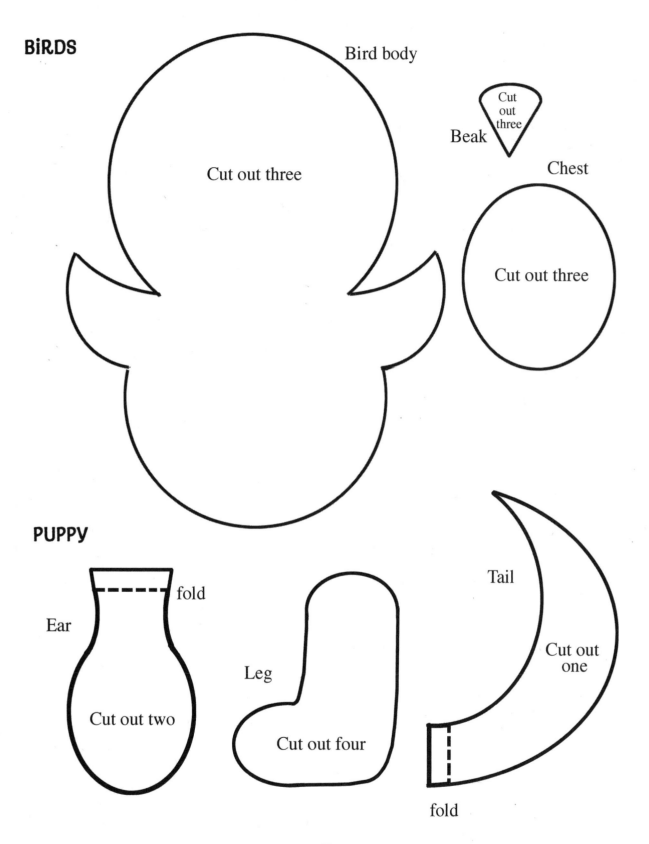

BiRDS

Bird body

Cut out three

Beak

Cut out three

Chest

Cut out three

PUPPY

fold

Ear

Cut out two

Leg

Cut out four

Tail

Cut out one

fold

3

PAPER PLATE BARNYARD ANIMALS

What you need:

9- and 7-inch paper plates
construction paper or foam
yarn
cotton balls
pipe cleaner
child's handprints for
    chicken comb and
    feathers
buttons or wiggle eyes
scissors
glue or tape

What to do:

Horse
1. Using the patterns on page 7, cut one head,
   two nostrils, two inner ears, and four legs and
   hooves from construction paper or foam.
2. Each child can color the paper plate or use the paper plate as a template
   to cut a 9 inch circle using construction paper or foam. This circle can
   then be glued on to the paper plate.
3. Glue the hooves to the legs and glue the legs to the back of the paper plate.
4. Glue the horse head to the front of the plate, glue on two pink nostrils and
   two pink ears. Add eyes using buttons or wiggle eyes.
5. Cut several pieces of yarn into 6-inch lengths and glue to the back of
   the plate for the tail. Cut several 3-inch strips of yarn and glue to
   the back of the head for the mane. Fluff the yarn forward.

Cow and Pig (Patterns on pages 9 and 13)
    The directions above also work to make the cow. Add some spots!

    For the pig, use a 7-inch paper plate for the pig's head. Glue on the pieces.
    Use a pink pipe cleaner to make the pig's tail curl and glue it to the back of
    the plate.

PAPER PLATE BARNYARD ANIMALS

Lamb
1. Cut out the patterns on page 11 using construction paper or foam.
2. Use the leg pattern provided on page 7 to cut out four legs and hooves. Glue the hooves to the legs and glue the legs to the back of the plate.
3. Glue the tail to the back of the plate.
4. Glue the lamb head to the front of the plate, then glue on a pink nose and two pink ears. Glue the wool to the top of the head and glue on the eyes.
5. Glue fluffy cotton balls to the lamb's body.

Chicken
1. Glue a 7-inch plate to the top of a 9-inch plate.
2. Using the patterns on page 13, cut out two legs using construction paper or foam and glue them to the back of the 9-inch plate.
3. Glue the beak and wattle onto the 7-inch plate and glue on the eyes.
4. Trace around the child's hand to create the feathers and red comb on some constructions paper or foam. Cut out and glue to the back of the plates as shown.

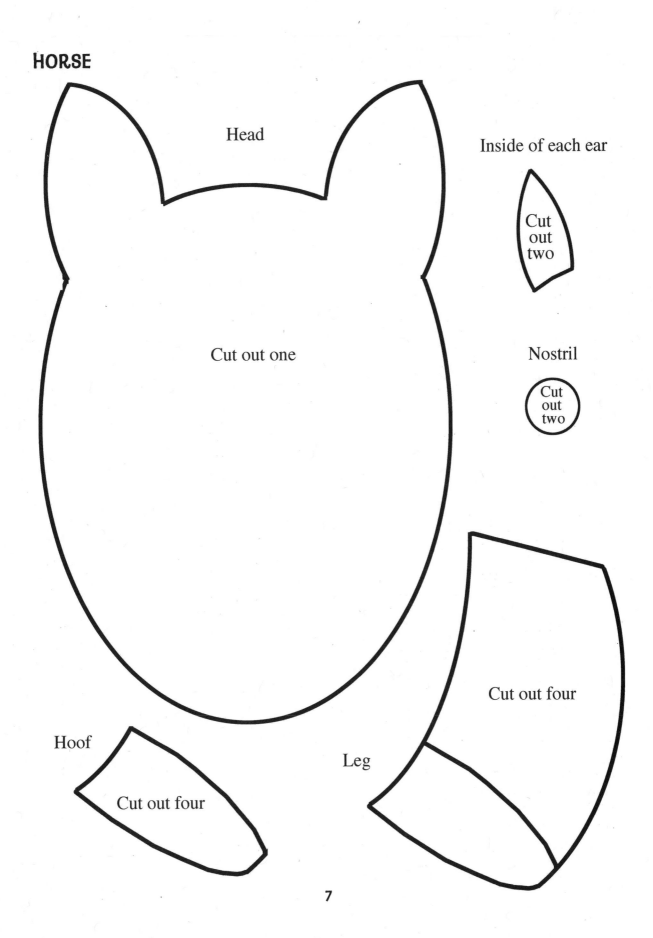

HORSE

Head

Inside of each ear

Cut out two

Cut out one

Nostril

Cut out two

Cut out four

Hoof

Leg

Cut out four

7

COW

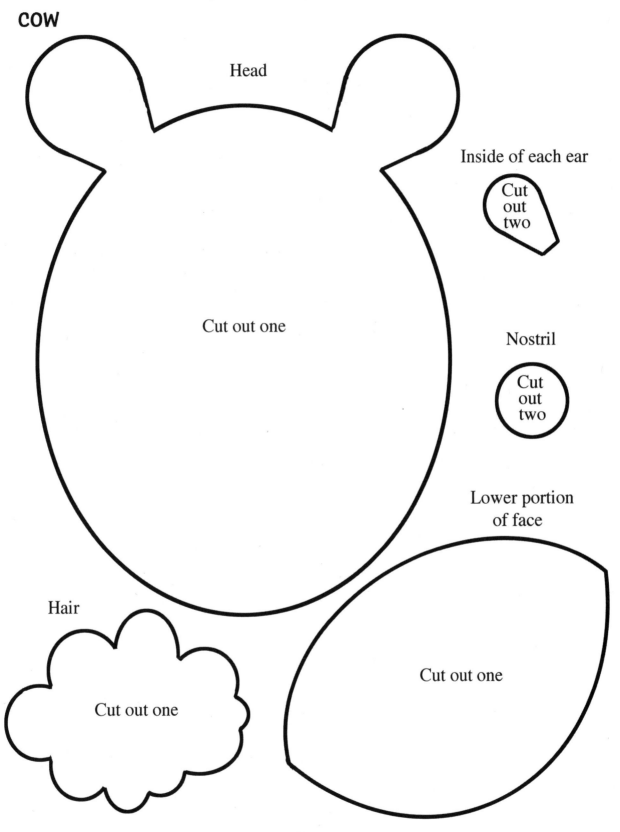

Head

Inside of each ear

Cut out two

Cut out one

Nostril

Cut out two

Lower portion of face

Cut out one

Hair

Cut out one

9

LAMB

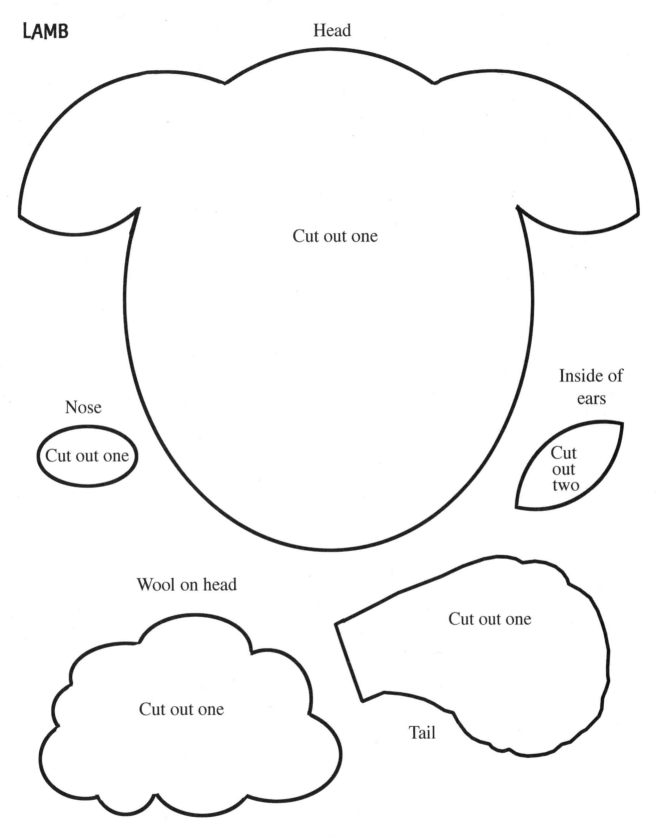

Head

Cut out one

Nose

Cut out one

Inside of ears

Cut
out
two

Wool on head

Cut out one

Cut out one

Tail

11

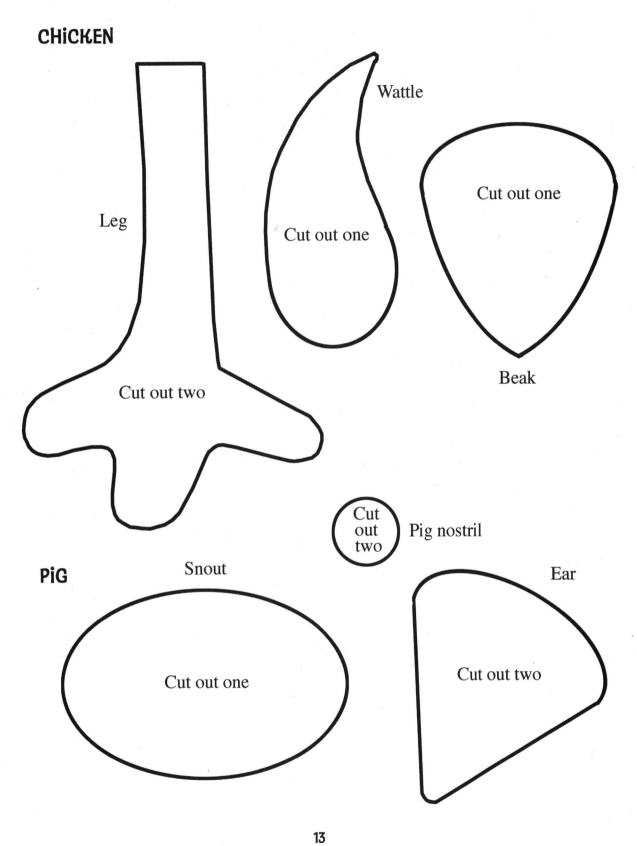

CHiCKEN

Leg

Cut out two

Wattle

Cut out one

Cut out one

Beak

Cut
out
two

Pig nostril

PiG

Snout

Cut out one

Ear

Cut out two

13

FLYING SAUCER

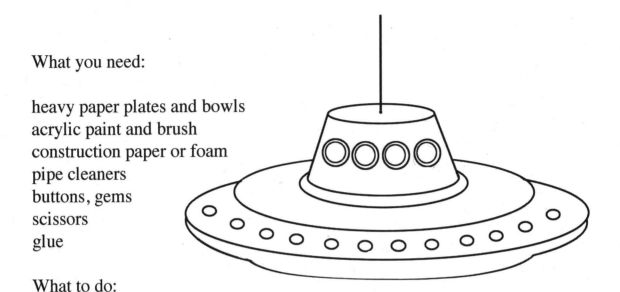

What you need:

heavy paper plates and bowls
acrylic paint and brush
construction paper or foam
pipe cleaners
buttons, gems
scissors
glue

What to do:

1. Paint the back sides of two paper plates. Silver paint is a great color to use for this step. Let the plates dry.
2. With the silver sides both facing out, glue the rims of the plates together as in figure 1.
3. Paint the back side of a paper soup bowl and let it dry.
4. For hanging, poke a hole in the middle of the bowl. Thread some yarn or string through the hole and tie a knot inside the bowl. Add glue to hold it in place.
5. Turn the bowl upside down, and glue to the top of the paper plate as shown in figure 2.
6. Add buttons or gems to decorate the spaceship.

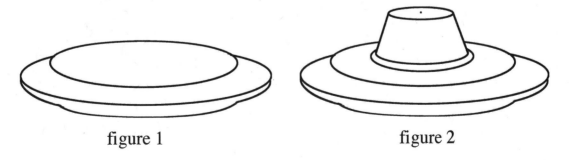

figure 1   figure 2

WATERMELON SLiCE

What you need:

one 9-inch paper plate
green and red construction
    paper
black marker
buttons
scissors
glue

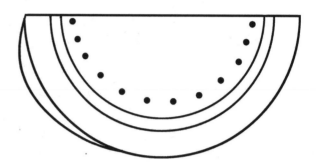

What to do:

1. Reproduce and cut out two each of the melon rind and inside patterns on page 17 using green and red construction paper.
2. Fold the paper plate in half so it will stand as in figure 1.
3. Glue the green construction paper cutout to the outside edge of the plate. Turn the plate over and glue the second green piece on the opposite side of plate.
4. Glue the red construction paper at the top of the fold on both sides. This will leave a white space separating the two colors.
5. Use a black marker to draw seeds on the melon or glue on buttons to use as seeds.

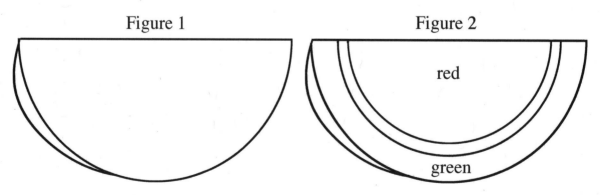

Figure 1

Figure 2

red

green

WATERMELON

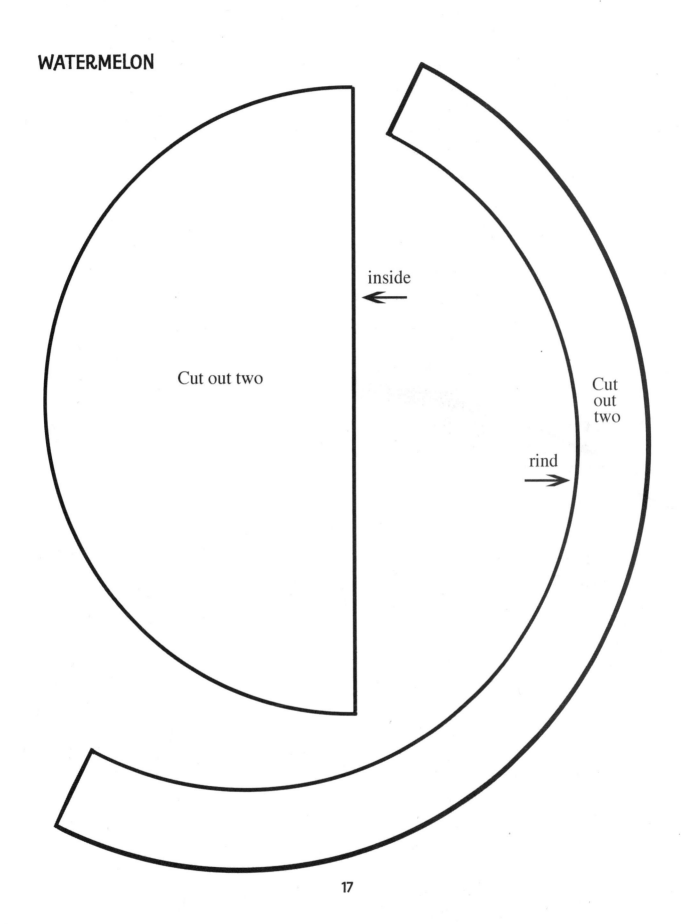

inside

Cut out two

Cut
out
two

rind

RECYCLED ROBOTS

This is a great project for a treasure hunt around the house. Collect all kinds of materials that could be used to make a robot.

What you need:

cans
plastic bottles   paper tubes
plastic lids   popcicle sticks
pipe cleaners   aluminum foil
buttons   bottle caps
corks   scissors
straws   glue or tape
toothpaste caps   small boxes
construction paper or foam
plastic or paper cups

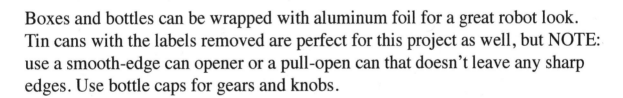

What to do:

Boxes and bottles can be wrapped with aluminum foil for a great robot look. Tin cans with the labels removed are perfect for this project as well, but NOTE: use a smooth-edge can opener or a pull-open can that doesn't leave any sharp edges. Use bottle caps for gears and knobs.

Buttons can be glued on for eyes or other decorations.

Corks and toothpaste caps make great robot legs or feet.

Lids and paper or plastic cups turned upside down make a great robot head as in the picture.

This project can be great fun for kids to build their own personal robot. Ideas are limitless. Just have fun!

FiSH AND TURTLE COMPACT DiSC

What you need:

two compact discs (CDs)
construction paper, cardstock or foam in a
    variety of colors
wiggle eyes or buttons
scissors
string or yarn
decoration ideas: cut out paper shapes, stickers,
    beads, buttons or gems, glitter

What to do:

1. Cut out the pieces for the fish and turtle
   on page 21 using construction paper,
   cardstock or foam.
2. Glue cutouts to the shiny side of the CD as
   shown in figure 1.
3. Decide how much string or yarn you will need to hang your fish or turtle
   and double it. Tie the ends together and glue to the side of the CD with
   the pattern pieces glued to it.
4. Glue the dull side of the second CD to the dull side of the CD with the
   patterns as shown in figure 2. Shiny sides of both CDs face outwards.
5. Add your choice of decorations.

figure 1　　　　　　　　figure 2

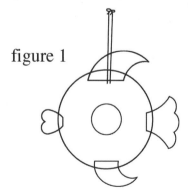
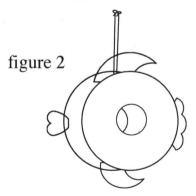

FiSH

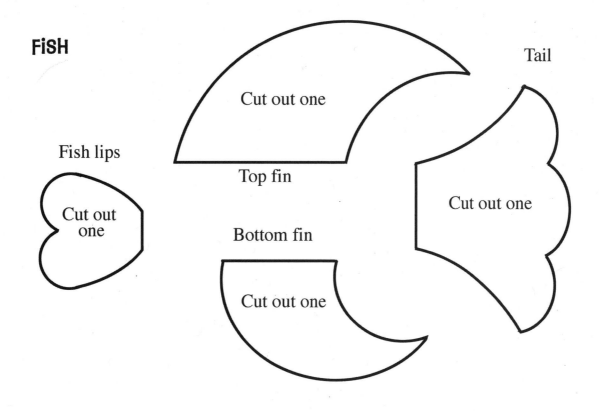

Fish lips

Cut out one

Cut out one

Top fin

Bottom fin

Cut out one

Cut out one

Tail

Cut out one

TURTLE

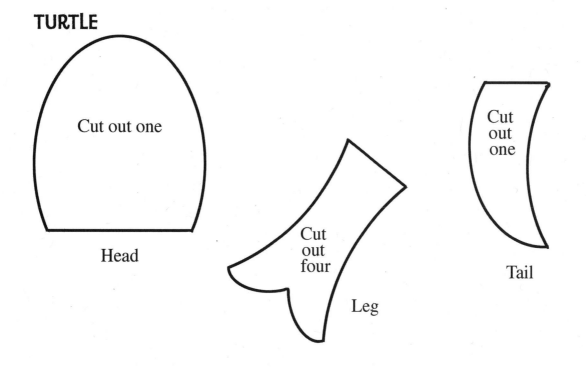

Cut out one

Head

Cut out four

Leg

Cut out one

Tail

PINE CONE OWL

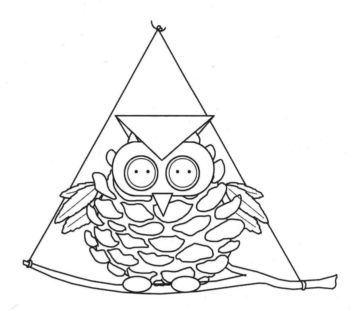

What you need:

pine cone for body
small twig
felt
buttons or wiggle eyes
yarn
feathers (optional)
glue
scissors

What to do:

1. Cut a strip of felt 1-1/2 inches by 3 inches and round the ends as shown in figure 1. Glue onto the owl.
2. Cut out and glue a small triangle for the beak as shown in figure 2. Glue on the eyes.
3. Cut out a 3 inch by 3 inch square of felt and fold in half. Glue one side to the front of the owl and glue the other side to the back as shown in figure 3.
4. Cut out approximately one-inch ovals for the feet and glue as shown in figure 4.
5. Decorate the owl with or without feathers.
6. Glue the owl to the twig. Let the glue dry.
7. Tie two pieces of yarn on the ends of the twig and tie for hanging.

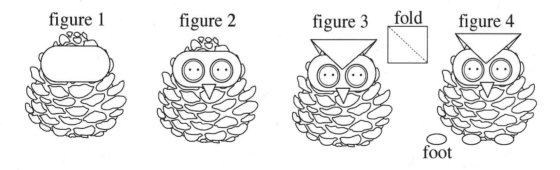

figure 1   figure 2   figure 3   fold   figure 4

foot

CLOTHESPIN SAFARI ANIMALS

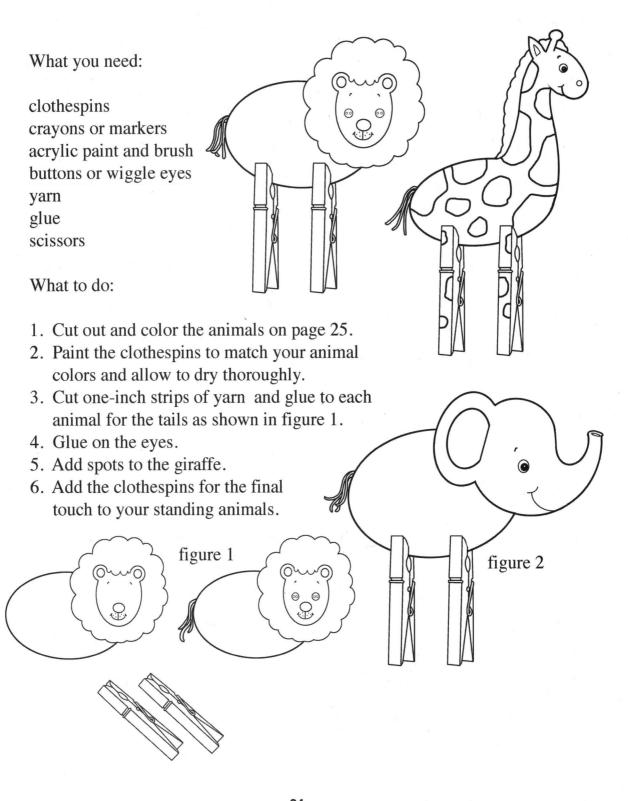

What you need:

clothespins
crayons or markers
acrylic paint and brush
buttons or wiggle eyes
yarn
glue
scissors

What to do:

1. Cut out and color the animals on page 25.
2. Paint the clothespins to match your animal colors and allow to dry thoroughly.
3. Cut one-inch strips of yarn and glue to each animal for the tails as shown in figure 1.
4. Glue on the eyes.
5. Add spots to the giraffe.
6. Add the clothespins for the final touch to your standing animals.

figure 1

figure 2

CLOTHESPIN SAFARI
ANIMALS

SWEET CUPCAKE LINER FLOWERS

What you need:

colorful cupcake papers
popsicle sticks
green acrylic paint and brush
green construction paper
glue
magnets (optional)
decorations: buttons, pom-poms,
    gems, child's photo cut into a
    circular shape

What to do:

1. Paint a popsicle stick green and let it dry.
2. Glue a cupcake paper to the popsicle stick.
3. Cut out the two leaves and glue them to the back
   of the popsicle stick. Use the leaf patterns
   provided on page 29.
4. Glue decorations into the flower centers. A child's
   photo cut into a round shape would look great, too!
5. The flowers can be arranged and glued onto a sheet of
   construction paper or kept as single flowers.
6. The flowers could also be used as refrigerator magnets if you
   glue a small magnet to the back of the popsicle stick.

FLOWER GARDEN FENCE

What you need:

popsicle sticks
acrylic paint and brush
green pipe cleaners
sheet of construction paper:
    blue for background, yellow for
    the sun, green for the grass and a
    variety of colors for the flowers
decorations: colorful papers, cotton
    balls, buttons, gems, glitter

What to do:

1. Paint popsicle sticks white and let them
   dry thoroughly.
2. Cut out the sun, flowers, grass and leaf shapes
   from the patterns provided on page 29.
3. Glue the grass onto the background paper.
4. Glue the painted popsicle sticks onto the
   construction paper as shown in figure 1.
5. Cut the pipe cleaners into various sizes for the
   flower stems and glue each one to the fence as
   shown in figure 2.
6. Glue a flower to each stem.
7. Glue on the leaves and the sun.
8. Decorate the flower centers
   however you like!

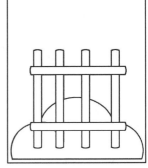

figure 1

figure 2

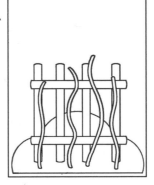

figure 3

FLOWER GARDEN FENCE AND LEAVES

Cut out one

Cut out one

CARDBOARD TUBE SNAKE

What you need:

several toilet paper tubes or paper towel tubes
string or yarn
buttons or wiggle eyes
acrylic paint and paint brush
hole punch
scissors
glue
red construction paper

What to do:

1. Cut several toilet paper rolls in half, paint and let them dry. You can also use paper towel tubes by cutting them into three or four sections.
2. Using a hole punch, punch two holes in the head and tail segments as shown in figure 1.
3. Punch four holes in the next few segments between the head and tail as shown in figure 2.
4. Thread the yarn through the head segment and tie to secure it as shown in figure 3. Begin threading the string through each segment like you are sewing or lacing it through, over and under as in figures 3 and 4. When you reach the tail segment, tie the yarn to secure it. Repeat steps on opposite sides of tubes.
5. Glue two eyes on the head segment.
6. Cut out a red tongue using two strips of construction paper and glue to the inside of the head.

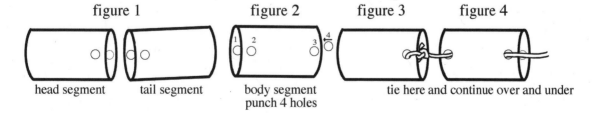

| figure 1 | figure 2 | figure 3 | figure 4 |

head segment   tail segment   body segment   tie here and continue over and under
                                punch 4 holes

FUNNY FROG PAPER PLATE

What you need:

9-inch paper plate
construction paper
black marker
green acrylic paint and brush
glue
tape
scissors

What to do:

1. Paint a 9-inch paper plate green. Let it dry.
2. Cut two legs and two hands using the patterns on page 33.
3. Cut two eyes using white construction paper. Cut two small circles for the eye dots, color them black or use black contruction paper, and glue them to the white construction paper.
4. Glue or tape the legs and the hands to the back of the paper plate as shown in figure 1.
5. Glue the eyes to the top on the front of the paper plate.
6. Use a black marker to draw a big smile for the frog.
7. Cut a strip of pink or red paper one inch long and six inches wide and glue to the smile. Roll the end of the tongue as shown in figure 2.

figure 1

figure 2

FROG

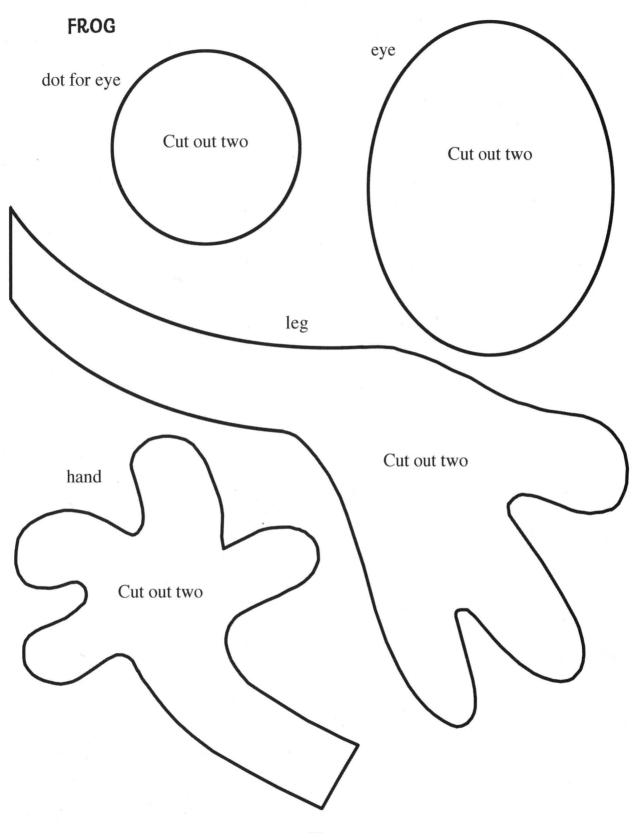

dot for eye

Cut out two

eye

Cut out two

leg

Cut out two

hand

Cut out two

33

EGG CARTON BUGS

What you need:

egg carton
pipe cleaners
buttons or wiggle eyes
acrylic paint and brush
pom-poms or other decorations
hole punch or pointed object
scissors
glue

What to do:

1. Cut apart an egg carton into individual cups.
2. Punch or poke three holes on opposite sides for the pipe cleaner legs as shown in figure 1.
3. Paint the outside of the cup any color and allow to dry.
4. To make the bug legs, cut a pipe cleaner into three sections and insert one section into each punched hole. Crimp the end of the pipe cleaner so it will stay in place. A bit of glue applied to the pipe cleaner will also help hold it in place.
5. Add buttons or wiggle eyes.

Bug

figure 1

figure 2

If you make a spider, make sure it has eight legs instead of six.

LADYBUG

Ladybug

1. Poke two holes in the egg cup as shown.
2. Paint and allow to dry. Add spots.
3. Cut a pipe cleaner in half for the antenna. Attach as in the bug instructions above.
4. Glue on a pom-pom for the head and add on the eyes.

SKY MOBILE

What you need:

aluminum pie tin or paper plate
cardstock or construction paper
yarn
buttons or wiggle eyes
scissors
hole punch to poke holes in tin or plate
crayon or marker

What to do:

1. Have an adult use a hole punch or a pointed object to poke five holes around the outside edge of the tin or plate as shown in figure 1. Punch one hole in the center of the plate.
2. Cut out the pieces on page 37 using cardstock or construction paper and add faces using buttons or wiggle eyes.
3. Use a hole punch to create a hole in the top of each pattern as shown in figure 2.
4. String yarn in various lengths through each pattern and tie as shown in figure 3.
5. Tie each pattern to the tin or plate as in figure 4. Tie a knot on top of each string to hold the pieces in place.
6. Cut another piece of yarn eight inches long and double the length. String both ends of the yarn through the hole in the center and tie a knot for the hanger.

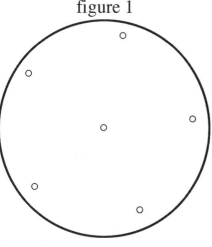

figure 1

figure 2

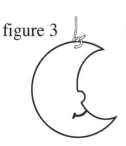

figure 3

figure 4

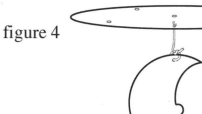

SKY MOBILE

Cut out one

Cut out one

Cut out one

Cut out one

Cut out one

MILK CARTON PUPPY

What you need:

milk or juice carton
construction paper or cardstock
cotton balls or pom-poms
buttons or wiggle eyes
pipe cleaners
scissors
glue or tape

What to do:

1. Have an adult cut the milk carton in half.
2. Cut a piece of construction paper long enough to wrap around all four sides of the carton and glue or tape as shown in figure 1.
3. Cut out the pieces using the patterns on page 41. You will need two ears.
4. Fold and glue the ears to the inside of the carton as shown in figure 2.
5. Cut two pipe cleaners in half for the whiskers. Glue to the carton as shown in figure 3.
6. Glue on the nose, tongue, and eye spot as shown in figure 4.
7. Glue on cotton balls or pom-poms to make the furry puppy muzzle as shown in figure 5 and add the eyes.
8. Cut a strip of paper or cardstock 1-1/2 inches wide and 12 inches long and glue to the inside of the carton to create a handle as shown above.
9. Glue on the folded part and attach the tail to the back of the puppy.

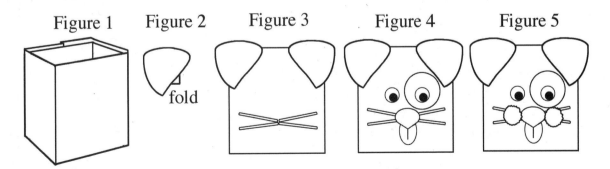

Figure 1   Figure 2   Figure 3   Figure 4   Figure 5

fold

GLASS JAR ANIMALS

What you need:

glass jars, various sizes
cotton balls or pom-poms
buttons or wiggle eyes
construction paper or foam
    in a variety of colors
pipe cleaners, yarn,
    or toothpicks
glue
tape
scissors

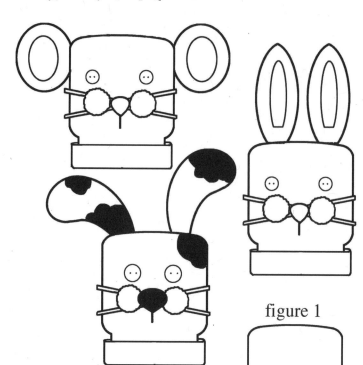

What to do:

1. Cut out pieces using the patterns on page 41. You will need two ears.
2. Glue a strip of paper or felt around the jar lid as shown in figure 1, and turn the jar upside down.
3. Fill each jar with strips of torn construction paper or foam for each animal's color. For the bunny, you can use cotton balls to fill the jar.
4 Cut yarn or pipe cleaners for the whiskers and glue to the front of the jar as shown in figure 2. Toothpicks could also be used as whiskers.
5. Glue on the nose.
6. Glue two pieces of cotton or pom-poms on top of the whiskers as shown in figure 3.
7. Glue the pink insides of ears to the outside of the ears. Glue the ears on the fold and attach them to the jar.
8. Glue on the eyes and decorate.

figure 1

glue or tape

figure 2

figure 3

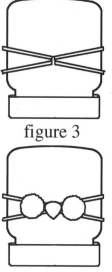

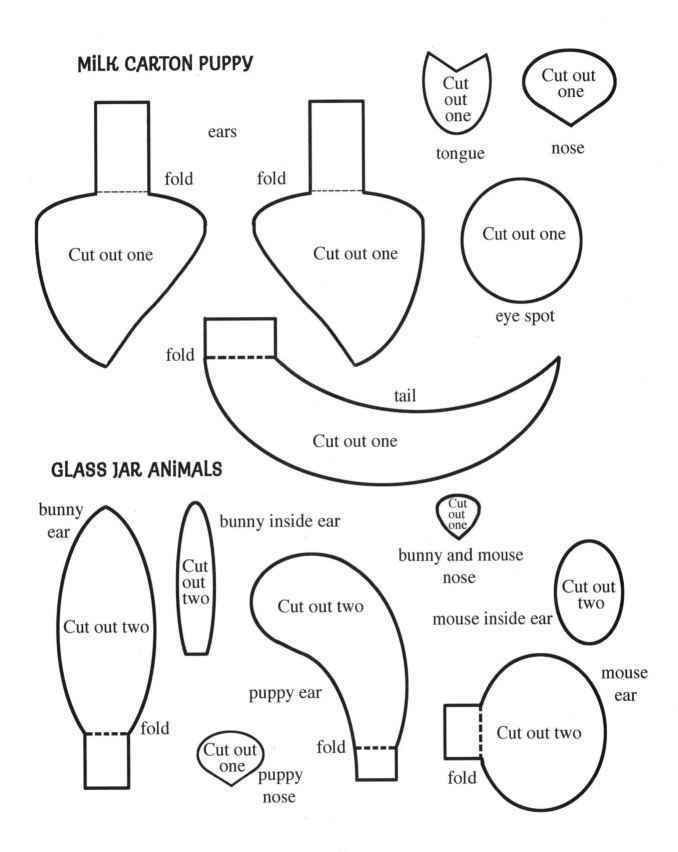

MiLK CARTON PUPPY

ears

fold

Cut out one

fold

Cut out one

Cut out one
tongue

Cut out one
nose

Cut out one
eye spot

fold

tail

Cut out one

GLASS JAR ANiMALS

bunny ear

Cut out two

bunny inside ear

Cut out two

Cut out one
bunny and mouse nose

mouse inside ear

Cut out two

Cut out two

puppy ear

fold

Cut out two

fold

Cut out one
puppy nose

fold

mouse ear

Cut out two

fold

41

PET ROCKS

What you need:

rocks of all shapes and sizes
acrylic paint and brush
markers
glue
buttons or wiggle eyes
decorations: pipe cleaners, yarn
    gems, stickers, glitter, pom-poms
construction paper or foam

What to do:

1. Clean the rocks in warm water with soap and let them dry.
2. Use your imagination to create your own special kind of pet. The rocks can be aliens, pet mice, dogs, cats, a paperweight for Mom or Dad or someone special. The possibilities are endless.
3. Smooth flat rocks work great for animals, along with smaller flat rocks for ears or feet, or maybe a nose.
4. Paint the rock and allow it to dry thoroughly.
5. To make an alien or monster, use any shape rock. Cut a pipe cleaner in small sections and glue to the rock for arms or antennas. Small, flat rocks can be used as feet. Glue on button or wiggle eyes. Use a marker to draw on the mouth. Paint stripes, dots or wiggly lines
6. Make a dog or cat by using a smooth, flat rock. Glue on ear-shaped rocks and a more round, tiny rock for the nose. Use paper, foam or yarn to add a tail or other features.
7. Make a rock self-portrait. Paint the rock, glue on small pieces of yarn for hair. Add buttons or wiggle eyes.
8. Paint the rock with dots, stripes, or wiggly lines, using fun colors. Use a marker to add your name. Add glitter, gems, stickers, or other decorations. Be creative and have fun!

PAPER BAG PUPPETS

What you need:

paper lunch bags
construction paper
child's handprint for owl wings
buttons or wiggle eyes
cotton balls or pom-poms
pipe cleaners or toothpicks
scissors
glue
crayons or maarkers

figure 1

What to do:

1. Cut out the pieces using patterns on page 45.
2. Have the child trace around a hand four times on construction paper. Cut out for the owl wings.
3. With the bottom of the paper bag facing you, glue on the ears, eyes and beak of the owl to the bag as shown to the right.
4. Glue on the handprint feathers as shown in figure 1.
5. Glue on the feet.
6. Decorate the owl with crayons or markers.
7. Cut two pipe cleaners in half and glue as shown for the kitty whiskers. Toothpicks can also be used for kitty whiskers.
8. Glue cotton balls or pom-poms on top of the pipe cleaners to make a cute furry face. Glue on the nose and eyes.
9. Glue the kitty ears to the top of the bag.
10. Glue on the tail as shown in figure 2.

figure 2

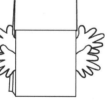

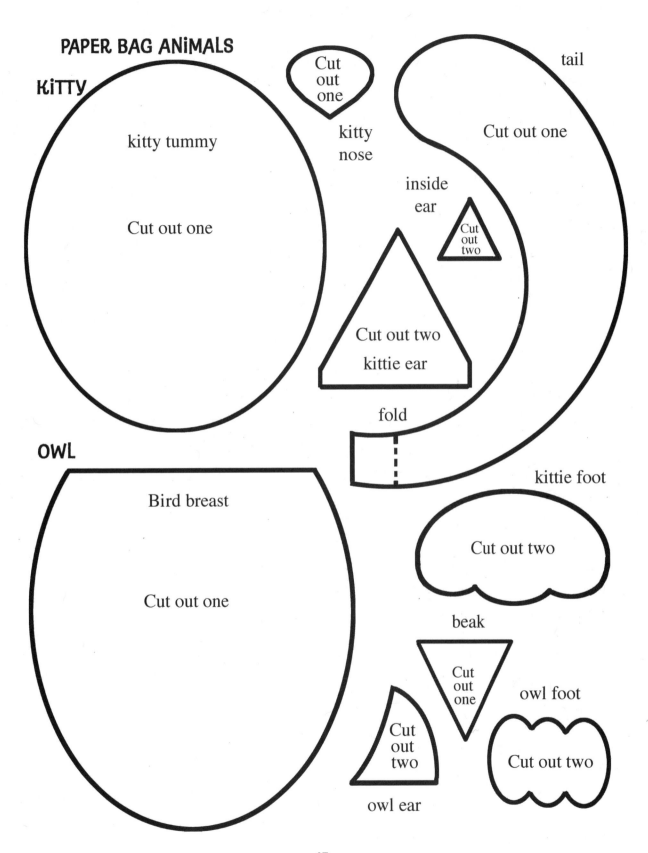

PAPER BAG ANIMALS

KiTTY

kitty tummy

Cut out one

Cut out one

kitty nose

tail

Cut out one

inside ear

Cut out two

Cut out two

kittie ear

fold

kittie foot

OWL

Bird breast

Cut out one

Cut out two

beak

Cut out one

owl foot

Cut out two

owl ear

Cut out two

45

TRAIN ON THE TRACKS

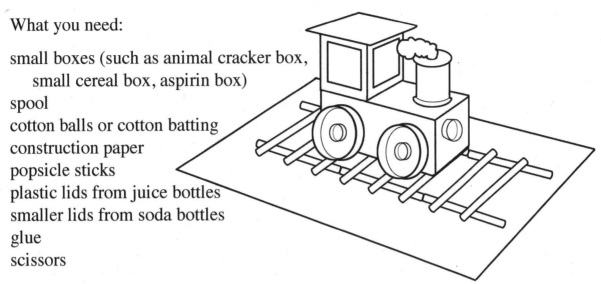

What you need:

small boxes (such as animal cracker box,
    small cereal box, aspirin box)
spool
cotton balls or cotton batting
construction paper
popsicle sticks
plastic lids from juice bottles
smaller lids from soda bottles
glue
scissors

What to do:

1. Tape two boxes together and cover them with construction paper as
   shown in figure 1.
2. Cut construction paper squares for the windows of the train and glue
   as shown in figure 2. Cut out and glue a piece of construction paper
   slightly larger than the top of the train and glue in place on top of the
   box. A child's photo could also be glued to the window of the train.
3. Glue on four juice lids for the wheels as shown in figure 3.
4. Glue on a small plastic lid for the light on the front of the train.
5. As shown in figure 4, glue on the spool and add some glue to the top
   of the spool. Glue on cotton balls or batting and pull it out to make it
   look like steam.
6. Glue green construction paper to cardboard and trim. Glue on popsicle
   sticks for railroad tracks as shown in figure 5. The number of popsicle
   sticks required will depend on the size of the train. Measure the width of
   the train and glue on the sticks based on the measurement.

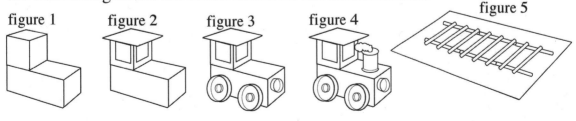

figure 1   figure 2   figure 3   figure 4   figure 5

PAPER TOWEL TUBE ROCKET

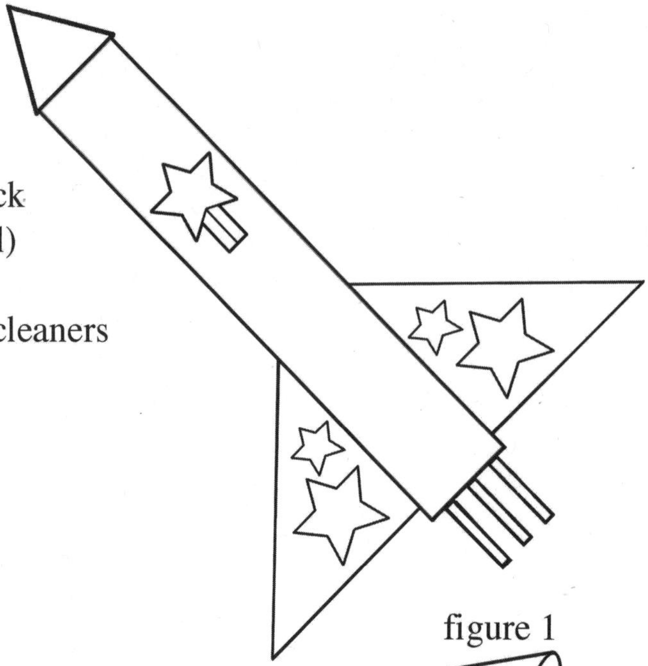

What you need:

paper towel tube
construction paper or cardstock
paint and paintbrush (optional)
crayons
red, orange, and yellow pipe cleaners
aluminum foil (optional)
glue
tape
scissors

What to do:

1. Cut a rocket nose out of construction paper or cardstock using the pattern on page 49. Cut a slit where indicated and roll into a cone. Tape as shown in figure 1.
2. Tape the cone to the paper towel tube.
3. The tube can be painted or wrapped with construction paper or aluminum foil. Glue and secure the paper or foil with tape.
4. Cut out two wings using the pattern on page 49. Glue the wings on the lower end of the tube as shown in figure 2.
5. Cut pipe cleaners in 2- to 3-inch lengths and glue and tape to the inside of the tube as shown in figure 3. This will serve as the rocket ignition fire.
6. Decorate with stickers, stars, or gems, or color with paint or crayons.

figure 1

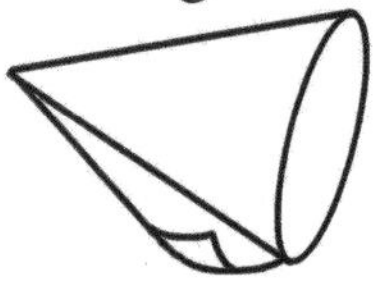

figure 2

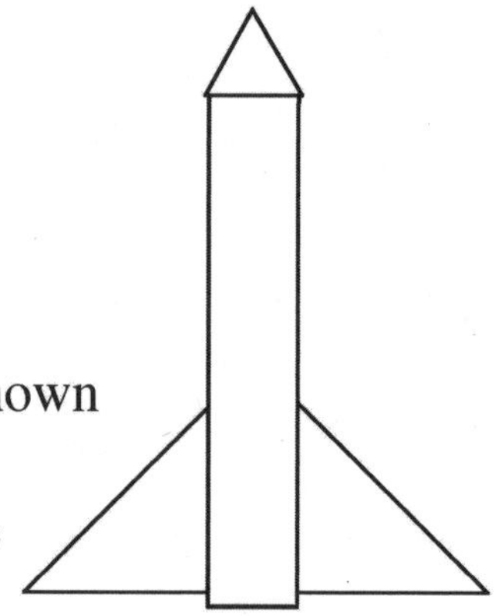

figure 3

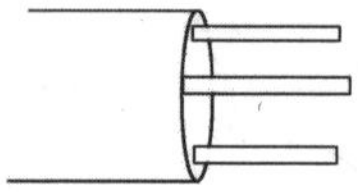

PAPER TOWEL ROCKET

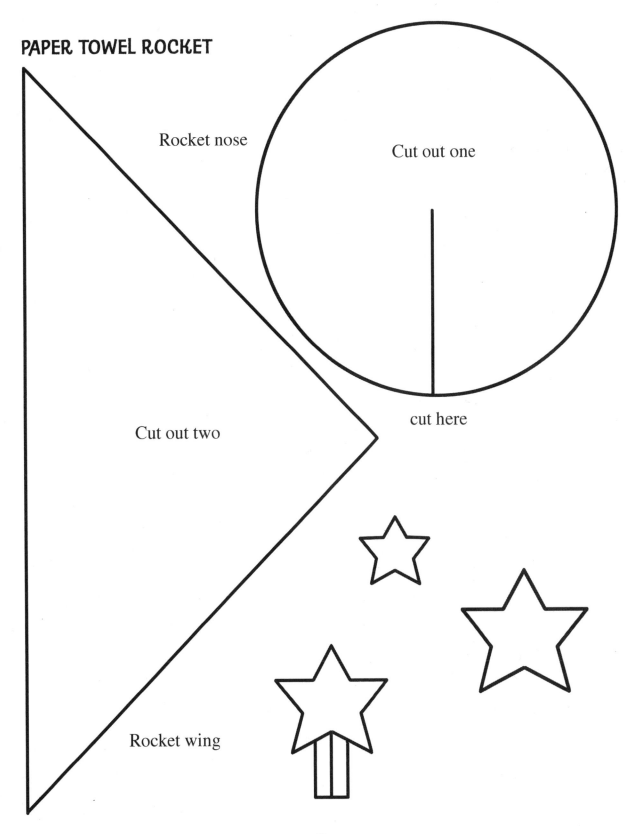

Rocket nose

Cut out one

cut here

Cut out two

Rocket wing

CATERPILLAR AND FROG EGG CARTON

What you need:

egg carton
pipe cleaners
buttons or wiggle eyes
acrylic paint and brush
pom-poms or other
    decorations
construction paper
hole punch or pointed object
scissors
glue

What to do:

1. Cut an egg carton into a strip of six egg cups.
2. Punch two holes in the top of the first egg cup.
3. Paint the egg carton strip and allow it to dry.
4. Cut a pipe cleaner in half and insert through the holes in the
   first egg cup, adding glue to the pipe cleaners inside the cup.
5. Glue on the eyes.
6. Decorate any way you like!

figure 1

FROG
1. Paint two egg cups and let them dry.
2. Glue the two cups together as shown in
   figure 1.
3. Cut a strip of pink or red construction paper
   one quarter inch wide and 2 inches long and glue between the
   cups where they meet. Roll the tongue as shown.
4. Glue on the eyes.
5. Cut out and then glue on the feet using the pattern on page 53.

TUBE BUTTERFLY AND DRAGONFLY

What you need:

toilet paper tube
pipe cleaners
crayons or markers
buttons or wiggle eyes
colorful papers or construction paper
   in a variety of colors
decorations: gems, glitter, buttons,
   crayons, markers
scissors
glue or tape

What to do:

1. Cover the tube with paper and glue or tape it to the tube.
2. Cut a pipe cleaner in half and glue or tape to the inside top of the tube as shown in figure 1.
3. Cut out two butterfly or dragonfly wings each using the patterns on page 53. Glue the wings to the side of the tube.
4. Glue on the eyes and add a smile using a marker or crayon.
5. Decorate any way you like!

figure 1

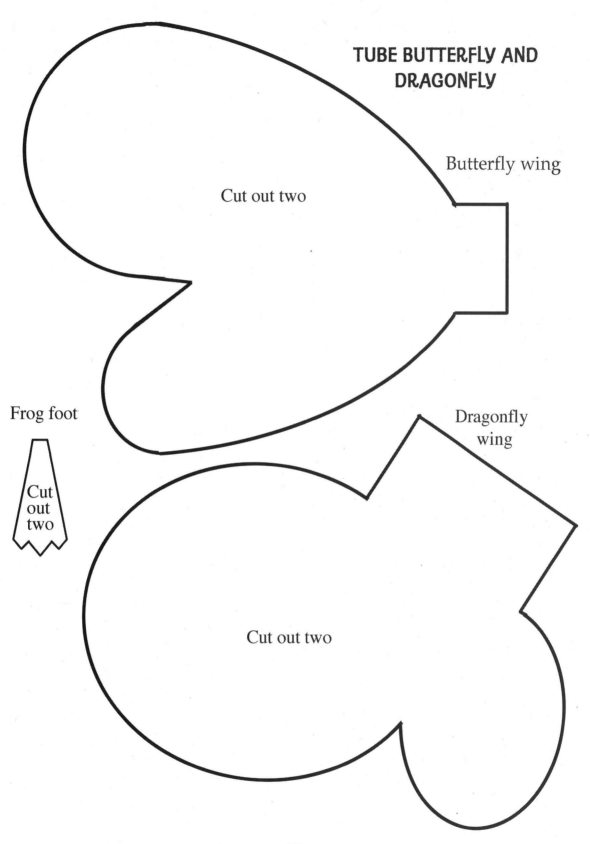

TUBE BUTTERFLY AND
DRAGONFLY

Butterfly wing

Cut out two

Frog foot

Cut
out
two

Dragonfly
wing

Cut out two

CLOTHESPIN NOTE HOLDERS

What you need:

clothespins
popsicle sticks
acrylic paint and brush
construction paper or foam
buttons or wiggle eyes
pipe cleaner

scissors
glue
magnets
decorations:
   gems, glitter,
   buttons

What to do:

1. Using the pattern on page 59, cut out the butterfly wings from construction papr or foam.
2. Paint the clothespins and let them dry.
3. For the butterfly (and the dragonfly), cut a pipe cleaner into four sections and glue two to the top side of the clothespin as shown in figure 1.
4. Glue the butterfly wings to the back of the clothespin and add the eyes.
5. To make the dragonfly, paint a clothespin and two popsicle sticks and let them dry.
6. Glue one popsicle stick on top of the other as shown in figure 2.
7. Glue the popsicle sticks to the back of the clothespin and add the eyes.
8. For the flower, cut out pieces using the patterns on page 59. Glue the largest flower on the front of the clothespin and glue the smaller flower on top of the larger flower. Add decorations.
9. For the elephant, cut out one head and two pink ears using the patterns on page 59 and glue to the head pattern as you can see above. Glue the elephant to the front of the clothespin and add the eyes.
10. Glue a magnet strip to the back of the clothespin and add a note!

figure 1   figure 2

BRACELET

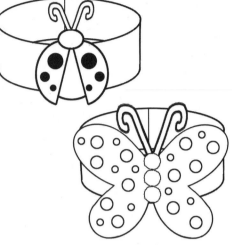

What you need:

cardstock or foam in a variety of colors
scissors
crayons, markers
glue or tape
decorations: pom-poms, gems, buttons,
    glitter, ribbon, or stickers

What to do:

1. Cut out a strip one inch wide and nine inches long out of construction paper or foam.
2. Cut out the flower, ladybug, or butterfly pieces using patterns on page 59 and glue to the bracelet.
3. For the flower bracelet, glue the largest flower on the bracelet first and then add the smaller one, using different colors.
3. Glue a pom-pom, button or other decoration to the flower center.
4. Repeat with the ladybug and butterfly patterns.
5. Help each child glue or tape the ends of their bracelets together to fit their wrists, leaving room to put it on or take it off easily.

You can also make an arm band for a superhero, or a secret spy decoder band or bracelet. Cut a wider strip, two inches wide, and decorate however you like!

tape here

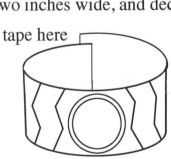

NECKLACE

What you need:

yarn or string; elastic string if available
cardstock or foam in a variety of colors
uncooked pasta (such as ziti, ditaliní, or
    penné)
acrylic paint and brush
colorful straws (optional)
scissors
decorations: glitter, gems, buttons

What to do:

1. For a pasta and flower combination necklace,
   paint the pasta in a variety of colors and allow to dry.
2. Cut out lots of flower pieces using the two patterns on page 59.
   Poke a small hole in the center of each flower for stringing.
3. Cut a piece of yarn or string about two feet long and tie
   a large knot at one end.
4. Decorate the flowers with glitter or other materials.
5. Thread the first flower and push it down to the knot. Begin to
   thread the pasta on to the necklace. Continue stringing the
   necklace by alternating pasta and flowers in any way you like.
6. When there are about three inches of string or yarn left, tie the ends
   together securely.
7. To use colorful straws in place of pasta, cut straws into approximately
   1 to 1-1/2 inches and thread alternately with the flowers.

SHOEBOX CORAL REEF

What you need:

shoebox
acrylic paint and brush
crayons or markers
cardstock or cardboard
sand if available
construction paper
seashells if available
glue
scissors

What to do:

1. Paint the inside and outside (optional) of the box blue. If sand is not available for the bottom of the reef, paint it a sand color, or cut a piece of sandy-colored construction paper and glue it to the bottom. If you use sand, add it after the coral, starfish, and octopus are in position.
2. Cut out and color the sea creatures on page 61.
3. Glue several kelp patterns on to the back wall of the box. For the coral, starfish, and octopus, make an L-shaped tab out of cardboard. Fold and attach to the bottom as shown in figures 1 and 2.
4. Use string to hang your fish and dolphin from the top of the box. Have an adult poke a hole in the top of the pattern and a hole in the top of the box. Attach and tie string, allowing the fish and dolphin to swim freely in the environment as shown in figure 3.
4. Add seashells if you have them.

figure 1   figure 2   figure 3

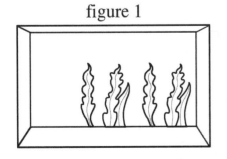

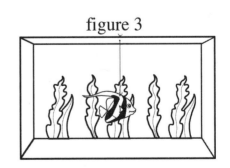

CLOTHESPIN NOTE HOLDERS, BRACELET, AND NECKLACE

Flowers

Ladybug

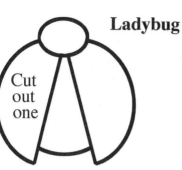

Cut out one

Clothespin
Butterfly
Wing
Y

Elephant head

Cut out one

Elephant ear

Cut out two

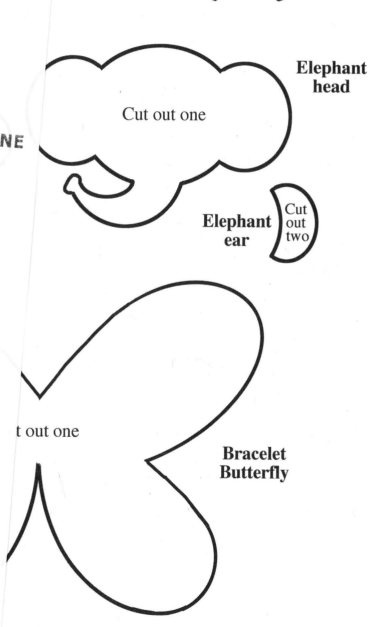

t out one

Bracelet Butterfly